What Willie Wore

What Willie Wore

Scenes from the Life & Wardrobe of a Very Fashionable Dog

by Alexander Stadler

CHRONICLE BOOKS
SAN FRANCISCO

Library of Congress Cataloging-in-Publication Data:
Stadler, Alexander.
What Wille wore: scenes from the life & wardrobe
of a very fashionable dog/by Alexander Stadler
p. cm.
ISBN 0-8118-3684-3
1. Dogs—Caricatures and cartoons. I. Title.
NC1429.S5698 A4 2003
741.5'973—dc21 2002074155

Manufactured in China.

Designed by Vanessa Dina

Distributed in Canada by Raincoast Books
9050 Shaughnessy Street
Vancouver, British Columbia V6P 6E5

10 9 8 7 6 5 4 3 2 1

Chronicle Books LLC
85 Second Street
San Francisco, California 94105

www.chroniclebooks.com

For the black dog and the white dog

Willie in a little
number from
Giorgio Armani

Backstage at Galliano

Off to Mica's
in Donna Karan

In a pearl gray shift
by Madame Grès

Willie on the runway
at Gucci

Hailing Audrey a cab
in Givenchy

Welcoming weekend guests
in Emilio Pucci

Exploring Graham technique
in Halston

Dancing on Avenue A
in Stephen Sprouse

Furniture shopping
in Hussein Chalayan

Denying the rumors
in Alexander McQueen

Showing off
the beautifully matched plaids
of her Pauline Trigère coat

Saying goodbye
to Carlo
in Balenciaga

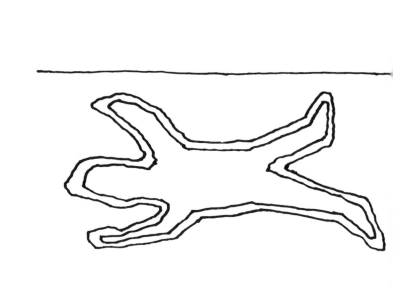

Scouting for the N.Y.P.D.
in Lily Daché

Listening to
Aerosmith
in Betsey Johnson

At Abbysinian Baptist Church
in Philip Treacy

Having a little
trouble breathing
in Mummy's Dior

Scrambling some eggs
for Catherine
in Yves Saint Laurent

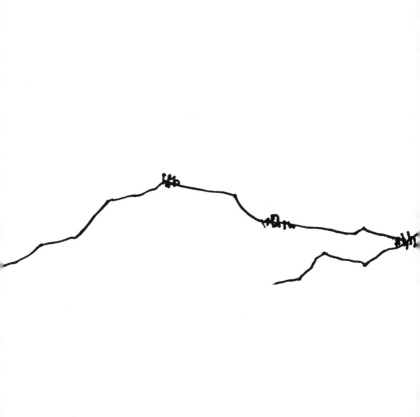

Wandering the moors
in Yohji Yamamoto

Having a vision
in Fortuny

Grocery shopping
for Diane
in Matsuda

Waiting for the bus
in Vivienne Westwood

Pitching a no-hitter
in Charles James

A quick coffee
in Geoffrey Beene

A Fitting at Vera Wang,
just in case

Shooting into orbit
in Paco Rabanne

Star gazing
in Sonia Rykiel

Dashing to the office
in Schiaparelli:

Waiting to be discovered
in Adrian

Popping a rivet
in Claire McCardell

Recovering from a mild flu
in Joan Vass

Subbing for Junior
in Anna Sui

Bringing Elizabeth
some fried chicken
in Roger Vivier

Helping Cher through it
in Bob Mackie

Gnawing on one
of Mr. Lipschitz's boots
from the early seventies

Lunch with Toukie
and the twins
in Willi Wear

Crashing the Perelman
Bas-Mitzvah in
Bill Blass

Two views
in Katherine Hamnett

Recovering from Paolo
in Vionnet

Blinding
half of Nashville
in Nudie Cohn

As mise-en-scène
at
the Gaultier Fall couture

On the road
with Marianne
in Ossie Clark

Willie in Jil Sander

Selecting peaches
for Marcella
in Valentino

Arguing with Isabella
in Zoran

Pumping iron
in Norma Kamali

Weaving
a tangled web
in Liz Collins

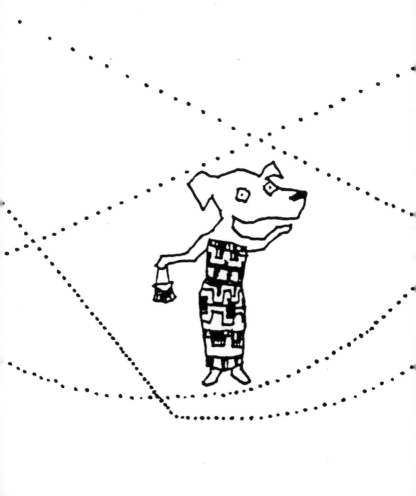

At one of those
big premieres with Susan
in Todd Oldham

At a museum benefit
in Commes des Garçons

Crossing the channel
in Lagerfeld

A pause
in Patou

In one of Tina's
Alaïas from
the late eighties

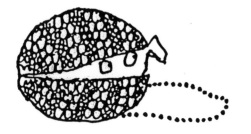

Hiding from
the paparazzi
in Judith Lieber

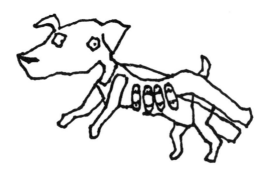

Hitting the clubs
in Versace

Showing Ivanka
how to work a pair of heels
in Thierry Mugler

Waiting for the Marquess
in Worth

Visiting
Ms. Davis
in Patrick Kelly

Willie
in Issey Miyake

Passing rumaki
in Jean Muir

Parachuting over Crete
in Manolo Blahnik

At a cocktail party
in the Hamptons
in
Isaac Mizrahi

Defending her thesis
in Chanel

Willie asleep on
a pillow from Calvin
Klein Home.